Weekend Walks South of Oxford

Short Scenic Strolls For All Ages
in South Oxfordshire

John Prior

Nine Peas Publishing

Published by Nine Peas Publishing

First published 2017
Updated and reprinted 2021

© John Prior 2021

All rights reserved. No part of this book may be reproduced in any form or by any means without the permission of the owner of the copyright.

All photographs © John Prior or Chris Preston

ISBN 978-0-9929688-4-7

Designed by Chris Preston

Typeset by Chris Preston

Printed by Press to Print Reading Ltd

Weekend Walks South of Oxford

Short Scenic Strolls For All Ages in South Oxfordshire

PUBLISHER'S NOTE

Whilst great care has been taken to provide information about the route, facilities and public transport for each walk that is accurate at the time of publication, the publisher cannot be held responsible for any inaccuracies or changes. However, feedback and updated information from readers is welcomed, for any future editions (email:ninepeaspublishing@btinternet.com). The sketch maps that accompany the walks show only the main paths, roads and buildings referred to in the route notes; Ordnance Survey maps provide fuller information. All distances are approximate.

Please note that this edition was prepared during the coronavirus pandemic, when the availability of public transport and facilities such as cafés was affected. Therefore checks for any future changes are recommended, using web-sites where available.

The cover photographs, clockwise from top left, are :
Henley Bridge (walk 6)
Butter Cross, West Hanney (walk 10)
Abingdon Weir (walk 1)
Watlington Hill (walk 12)
Dorchester Abbey (walk 2)
Near Ewelme (walk 5)

Symbols used on maps

Walk Start
Toilets
Café/Pub/Shop
Playground
Viewpoint
Railway Station

Contents

	Page
Introduction	1
Walk Locations	2

Walks

Abingdon (1¼ or 2 miles)	4
Dorchester-on-Thames (1¼ or 2 miles)	8
East Hagbourne (2 miles)	11
East Hendred (1¼ miles)	14
Ewelme (¾ mile or 2 miles)	17
Henley-on-Thames (2 miles)	20
South Stoke (2 miles)	23
Stadhampton (1¼ or 1¾ miles)	26
Stoke Row (1½ or 1¾ miles)	29
The Hanneys (1¾ miles)	32
Wallingford (1¼ or 1½ miles)	35
Watlington (¾ mile or 2 miles)	39

Further Information	42

DEDICATION
To my wife Anne, daughters Jo, Cathy and Sarah
and grandchildren Ben, Josh, Hannah, Ethan and Dylan.

ACKNOWLEDGEMENT and THANKS
To Chris for his patience and professionalism in
turning my typescript into this book.

Introduction

South Oxfordshire includes parts of the Thames Valley, the Chiltern Hills and the Vale of White Horse – a landscape of river valleys, wooded hills, market towns and picturesque villages, with much of it designated an 'area of outstanding natural beauty'. These 12 circular walks have been chosen for anyone who wants to get out into the fresh air for a short, interesting stroll in this beautiful part of England.

Each route is no more than 2 miles long, mainly level, and incorporates places of interest, stops for refreshments or a picnic and a children's playground. The starting points have been chosen for easy car parking and/or access by public transport. Numbers within the route descriptions link to facts and figures about the places passed.

The walks will suit families with children and anyone who wants some exercise for an hour or so in interesting surroundings. So pick a route and head off to discover the towns, villages and 'outstanding natural beauty' south of Oxford. Despite the title, it doesn't *have* to be at a weekend!

The author

For over 40 years I've lived in Pangbourne, where my wife Anne and I brought up our three daughters. It was they who originally inspired this book. At weekends we were keen to explore the local area but any walk had to be child-friendly – not too long and, if possible, including a playground and an ice-cream! So we collected suitable routes.

Our first collection of local walks was published in *Weekend Walks West of Reading* and this book contains a second collection. Being 'senior citizens' with five grandchildren, these walks were again chosen with both the young and the not-so-young in mind!

Walk Locations

WALK ONE : ABINGDON

Along the Thames and across a thundering weir to the remains of a great Abbey.

START/PARKING: Rye Farm car park (pay and display, 2 hours free) on the A415 just south of Abingdon Bridge (Nat Grid Ref 41/501968, Postcode OX14 3HP)
PUBLIC TRANSPORT: Thames Travel buses from Oxford, Didcot and Wallingford to Abingdon town centre
DISTANCE: 1¼ miles (2 km) or 2 miles (3¼ km)
REFRESHMENTS: Kiosk outside swimming pool, Abbey Meadows (seasonal); several cafes, coffee shops and pubs in Abingdon town centre including the Crown and Thistle in Bridge Street and the Nags Head at the bridge
PUBLIC TOILETS: Abbey Meadows (daily Apr to Sept, weekends Oct to March) and Hales Meadow car park (opposite Rye Farm car park)
PATHS: Mainly footpaths; level and suitable for pushchairs, but those near the Thames are liable to be muddy (or even flooded) after wet weather

THE ROUTES: For the longer route, at the car park entrance turn right along the lane towards Rye Farm. There are wide views across the fields of Andersey Island. By some cottages, continue ahead along a stony path past a metal gate. After crossing a small concrete bridge, take the grassy path across a field. Where this divides, take the path to the right over a wooden bridge (old railway sleepers). This leads to the Swift Ditch, the site of the first pound lock on the Thames ❶. There is an information panel just before a bridge over this fast-running stream. From here, retrace your steps to the fork in the paths and turn right across the field. This path leads to the Thames and to Abingdon Lock, from where the walk description is the same as the short route (see below).

For the short walk, at the car park entrance go into the adjacent meadow. Take the path ahead across the grass towards the Thames, then turn right to join the riverside path. There are benches, fine views of Abingdon Bridge and glimpses of Abingdon's historic buildings across the river – from left to right, St Helen's church spire, the imposing Gaol, County Hall with its white cupola and weather vane, and the Abbey buildings. Continue along the riverside to reach Abingdon Lock ❶, usually busy with boats in spring and summer. There is an information board and, on the lock-keeper's house, marks recording the floods of 1875, 1894 and 1947.

Carefully cross the lock gates, to pass information panels about 'paddle and rymer weirs' and the lock, then cross the weir with its thundering white water. Follow the shady path along the bank of the Mill Stream with its dabbling ducks. On the left are the Abbey Meadows, with a well-equipped children's playground suitable for primary and pre-school ages. Between this and an outdoor swimming pool is a children's water play area (seasonal). Turn right across the footbridge near the pool to enter the Abbey Gardens, the site of Abingdon Abbey ❷; there are information panels at the entrance. Follow the path to the left, towards a statue of Queen Victoria, to reach formal gardens with fine floral displays. From here take the path on the left towards a wall, where there is information

about this part of the Gardens. Go through the gate in the wall, turning left then immediately right into Checker Walk. This narrow lane leads to some of the surviving Abbey buildings – the Checker, Checker Hall and Long Gallery ❸ – with an information panel on the left. Go ahead through a narrow passage-way in the buildings to reach Thames Street then turn right, with the Mill Stream on your left and the Gaol ❹ ahead. At the end of the street Abingdon town centre, with its magnificent County Hall ❺, is a short distance to the right. To complete the walk, turn left into Bridge Street and cross the bridge to reach the car park.

Abbey Gateway

View towards St Helen's Church

County Hall

Abingdon Lock

Facts and Figures

❶ The first pound lock on the Thames was built in the early 1600s at the entrance to the Swift Ditch, the old course for boats – a 'short cut' avoiding Abingdon. The remains of this are the oldest surviving lock in the country. The first Abingdon Lock was built in 1790 and from then river traffic used today's route; the present lock dates from 1905.

❷ A monastery was first established on this site in the late 7th century. After a period of decline, from the 11th century it flourished again to become the great Benedictine Abbey of St Mary, larger than Westminster Abbey is today. This was demolished in the mid-1500s on the orders of Henry VIII and all the stone was removed - lines of paving in the gardens show where it once stood. However, a few of the domestic buildings of the Abbey survive (see 3).

❸ The mid-13th century Checker was the Abbey's Exchequer (counting house), and has a fine stone chimney. The adjacent Checker Hall is now a theatre. The Long Gallery, dating from the late1400s, was probably used by clerks and later as accommodation for visitors. The Abbey buildings are open to the public on Wednesday, Thursday and Sunday afternoons from May to September (www.friendsofabingdon.org.uk).

❹ The massive County Gaol was built in the early 1800s but closed in 1868 and the prisoners were transferred to Reading. It became a grain store, then a sports centre and has recently been converted into flats and restaurants.

❺ The handsome County Hall was built in 1678-82 as an assize court and market house. Abingdon was the county town of Berkshire from the mid-1500s to the mid-1800s, remaining in Berkshire until the 1974 local government re-organisation. County Hall now houses a local history museum, open Tue to Sun with free admission (www.abingdon.gov.uk). There is a long tradition of celebrating important events by the Mayor and councillors throwing currant buns from the roof to crowds in the Market Place. This was done on 11 June 2016 to mark the 90th birthday of Queen Elizabeth II and on 11 November 2018 to commemorate 100 years since the end of WW1.

WALK TWO : DORCHESTER-ON-THAMES

Through this picturesque village, with its magnificent Abbey, and across a water meadow to the hamlet of Overy (*Midsomer Murders* location).

START/PARKING: Dorchester lies off the A4074, about 10 miles SE of Oxford. The walk starts at the Recreation Ground, at the northern end of the High Street, where there is ample roadside parking in Oxford Road and Drayton Road (Nat Grid Ref 41/576948, Postcode OX10 7PJ)
PUBLIC TRANSPORT: Thames Travel buses Oxford-Wallingford-Reading/Henley stop on the Dorchester by-pass close to the start in Drayton Road
DISTANCE: 1¼ miles (2 km) or 2 miles (3¼ km)
REFRESHMENTS: Abbey Tea Room (afternoons from Easter to September, see www.dorchester-abbey.org.uk), the Fleur de Lys(FDL), George and White Hart pubs, Lily's Tea Room (closed Tues and Wed) and Co-op store (open daily) - all in the High Street
PUBLIC TOILETS: In Bridge End, at the southern end of the High Street.
PATHS: Footpaths and pavements, level but mainly unsuitable for pushchairs because of stiles and muddy stretches after wet weather

THE ROUTES: There is a children's playground at the Recreation Ground, suitable for primary and pre-school children. To begin the walk, continue along Drayton Road past Dorchester Lake and bungalows to reach an information board on the right, by a footpath. Take this path, which borders fields to the left and back gardens to the right. Follow this along the field edge to reach a bridge over the River Thame and go into the Hurst Water Meadow ❶. There is an information panel on the right, and the three paths from here all lead to a stile on the far side of the meadow. Follow the path beyond over a wooden bridge, past weather-boarded Overy Mill ❷ and the mill pond and over another stile. This leads to a narrow lane, then turn right into another lane to pass 18th century Overy Manor, Overy House and Overy Farmhouse. There is a fine view across the fields to the left towards the distant Chilterns. The lane leads to the eastern end of Dorchester Bridge ❹. For the shorter route, go over the bridge to reach the southern end of High Street and the former Toll House (see walk continuation on page 9).

For the longer route, carefully cross the road here and go through a kissing gate where there is an information panel about Old Bridge Meadow. Follow the grassy path ahead, with the meandering River Thame to the right and views of Wittenham Clumps. At the Thames, turn right and cross a wooden bridge over the River Thame, then follow the path that curves to the right beside the Thame. This soon leads past the low grassy mounds of the Dyke Hills ❸ stretching away to the left. The path veers to the right (past a WW2 pill box), then along a field edge towards the village. At the end of the path, go through a metal gate and take the stony lane to the right of a thatched cottage. At the end of this lane go ahead into a road towards the Church of St Birinus. This road, Bridge End, leads to the High Street.

Carefully cross the road to reach the former Toll House near the bridge ❹ and take the path here into the grounds of the Abbey ❺. This beautiful building is well worth visiting, with a museum and tea room in the former Abbey guest house nearby. To continue the walk, pass under the lych gate and turn right into the very attractive High Street with its fine houses, pretty cottages and former coaching inns (the Fleur de Lys, George and White Hart). Continue along the High Street to pass the village War Memorial and reach

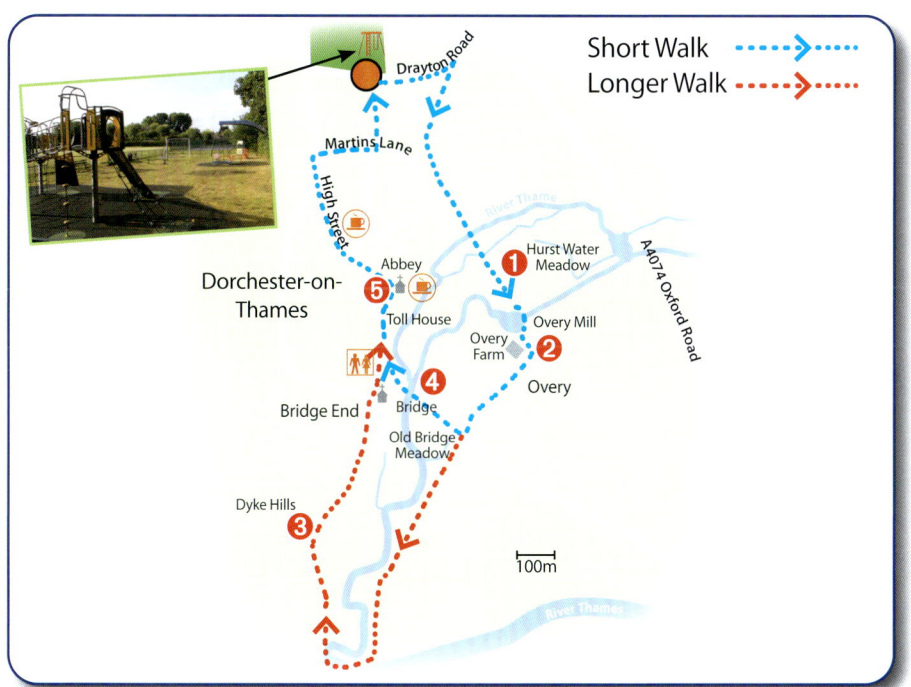

a fine thatched cob wall on the left. Turn right here into Martin's Lane and, at the junction with Queen Street, turn left along a path past the houses of Belcher Court. This path leads back to the Recreation Ground.

> **Facts and Figures**
>
> ❶ The 18 acre Hurst Water Meadow is managed by a Trust that also manages nearby Old Bridge Meadow and Overy Mead Piece (www.hurst-water-meadow.org.uk). The meadow was allowed to flood when the river flow was too high for Overy Mill.
>
> ❷ There have been mills here since at least the 11th century, powered by water from the River Thame diverted into a mill race. The present mill stopped grinding corn in the 1920s.
>
> ❸ The earthworks of the Dyke Hills are the remains of Iron Age defences. These consisted of two banks and a ditch between the rivers Thames and Thame, protecting a settlement. At the eastern end there are also five barrows, thought to be Bronze Age burial sites.
>
> ❹ The earliest evidence for a bridge over the River Thame is in the mid-12th century. The present one dates from 1813-15, built about 100m upstream from the earlier ones. Tolls were collected at the nearby Toll House until 1873.
>
> ❺ The Abbey church of St Peter and St Paul was established as an Augustinian monastery in the mid-12th century on the site of a Saxon cathedral. Among the many treasures are a Norman decorated font, medieval stone effigies and a stained glass window of the Tree of Jesse (www.dorchester-abbey.org.uk).

Abbey Museum

High Street

WALK THREE : EAST HAGBOURNE

A ramble along an old railway line and through this gem of a village.

START/PARKING: Recreation Ground in Great Mead, a turning off New Road (B4016) opposite Hagbourne Garage, with roadside parking (Nat Grid Ref 41/532886, Postcode OX11 9BN). There is alternative parking nearby, on the gravel track to the Millennium Wood.
PUBLIC TRANSPORT: Thames Travel bus route 94 from Didcot, Mon-Sat
DISTANCE: 2 miles (3¼ km)
REFRESHMENTS: At the Community Shop (open Mon-Fri to 4pm and Sat morning) and Fleur de Lys pub (www.thefleurdelyspub.co.uk)
PUBLIC TOILETS: None, but toilets at the Fleur de Lys for customers
PATHS: Level footpaths and pavements mainly suitable for pushchairs; some of the paths will be muddy after wet weather

THE ROUTE: At the Recreation Ground there is a playground for children up to 12 years old, seats and space for a picnic. From here, walk back along Great Mead to New Road and carefully cross this to the Community Shop. Turn right along New Road and shortly left along a wide gravel track signed 'Footpath to Didcot'. This leads to the Millennium Wood through a metal gate on the right, with an information panel. Follow the path ahead to reach a clearing with a circle of 12 stones. Bear left out of this clearing and at the edge of the wood, turn left then immediately right to join a path. Where another path crosses this, by a wooden sculpture, turn left. Mowbray Fields Local Nature Reserve lies to the right here. Continue ahead, following the route of a former railway line ❶. This very gradually rises on to an embankment to give wide views over East Hagbourne and the surrounding countryside towards the Berkshire Downs on the horizon.

The path crosses a bridge over the road between East and West Hagbourne. At a path junction about 400m beyond this, drop down the path to the left to reach another brick bridge. Turn right here on to a path between fields. This leads over a stream to a gravel drive, towards the tower of St Andrew's church ❷. Bear left through the churchyard and turn right into Church Close. Just ahead is a stone cross ❸ topped by a sundial. Carefully cross the road here and continue ahead along Main

Road, with its variety of attractive houses from the 15th, 16th and 17th centuries. Many have thatched roofs, timber frames or herring-bone brickwork. Shortly after the 17th century Fleur de Lys pub, a path to the right (signposted Footpath Parsonage Lane) runs between parts of a clear stream - Hacca's Brook ❹. After a detour down this shady path, continue along Main Road and take the next narrow path on the left (Bakers Lane). This becomes a stony track that leads round to the Community Shop and the start of the walk at Great Mead.

Millennium Wood

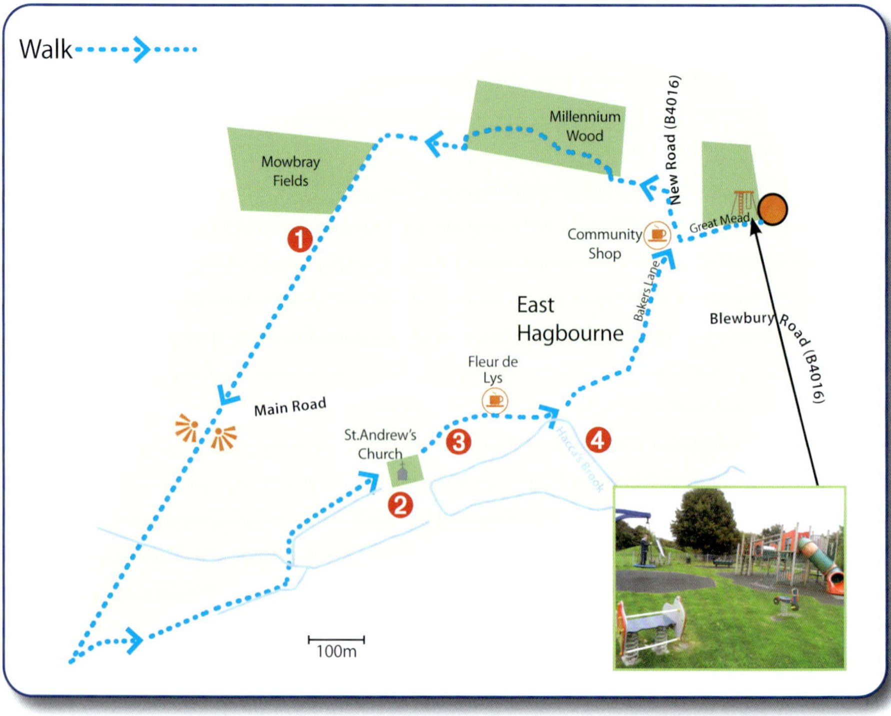

Facts and Figures

❶ This is the line of the former railway from Didcot to Newbury, opened in 1882 as part of a direct route from the Midlands to Southampton. During WW2 it was a crucial link for the movement of troops and military supplies, especially in the run-up to D-Day. Afterwards, a decline in passenger traffic resulted in closure in the early 1960s and the line was dismantled in 1967.

❷ The parish church of St Andrews was built, or re-built, in the early 12th century but only a few of these walls remain. There were later additions, including the tower in the mid-15th century. The church has many notable features, including a fine medieval pulpit and font.

❸ The 15th century Upper Cross is one of three ancient stone crosses, thought to mark an area of refuge. The others, now just stumps were next to the War Memorial at the eastern end of Main Road (the Lower Cross) and at Coscote on the road to West Hagbourne.

❹ The name of the village derives from Hacca (or Hakka), the 9th century chief of a West Saxon tribe. He settled in this area beside a stream that still bears his name – Hacca's Brook.

St. Andrew's Church

Upper Cross

WALK FOUR : EAST HENDRED

Step back in time with a stroll round this ancient village at the foot of the Berkshire Downs.

START/PARKING: East Hendred is just south of the A417 about 4 miles east of Wantage. There is roadside parking in High Street near St Augustine's church (Nat Grid Ref 41/459886, Postcode OX12 8LA)
PUBLIC TRANSPORT: Thames Travel buses from Wantage, Didcot, Abingdon and Oxford, Mon-Sat (X32 along A417; 33/X33 to Orchard Lane)
DISTANCE: 1¼ miles (2 km)
REFRESHMENTS: Hendred Stores (www.hendredstores.co.uk), the Wheatsheaf Inn (www.wheatsheafeasthendred.co.uk) and the Eyston Arms (www.eystonarms.co.uk)
PUBLIC TOILETS: None, but toilets at the pubs for customers
PATHS: Village roads and footpaths, mainly level and suitable for pushchairs

THE ROUTE: For a small village, East Hendred has an amazing collection of listed buildings, some dating back to the 1300s. The walk begins at the junction of High Street and Church Street. With the church behind you, cross the road and turn left into St Mary's Road. On your left are the grounds of Hendred House ❶ and ahead lies the RC parish church of St Mary's. Turn left at the church along a cobbled pavement to pass under an arch linking the church and presbytery; St Amand's RC school is close by to the right. Shortly, where the lane bears right, go ahead to join a 'restricted byway' past Cozens Farm. Follow the footpath, bearing left where the path divides and turning left where the path meets a track. This track rises gently through woodland to reach the corner of a large field. Turn sharp left here to join a track back into the woods. This track leads down between fields of the Hendred Estate and, after passing the brick buildings of the Old Estate Yard, turn right into High Street.

The High Street presents a very attractive scene of grassy banks, flower beds, old cottages and the Hendred Stores with its fine Elizabethan brickwork. There is an information panel about the village next to this. Continue along past the Eyston Arms pub to reach the thatched buildings of King's Manor and Barn, bordering Chapel Square. Cross the road near the war memorial to pass the Champs Chapel Museum ❷ and, just beyond on the right, the 16th century Wheatsheaf Inn. Here, cross the road and turn left into Cat Street past a thatched cob wall then Orchard House, the former home of scientist William Penney (note the blue plaque). Shortly, opposite The Old Cottage, join a footpath on the left. This leads through a metal kissing gate to a bench with a view across fields to the parish church. On the right at the bottom of the slope is the Penney Playpark ❸, with a range of play equipment for children up to 12 years and space for picnics. Note the fine carved owl, one of several around the village (an Owl Trail established in 2016). Just beyond on the right is Snells Hall, the former village school of 1860, now the village hall. At the end of the path, turn left into Church Street to reach St Augustine's church ❹. See if you can spot the stone head in the church wall (found as part of the rubble within the wall when it was recently renovated). The start of the walk is just past the church.

With grateful thanks to Tessa Case of East Hendred for her help with this walk and the village's history.

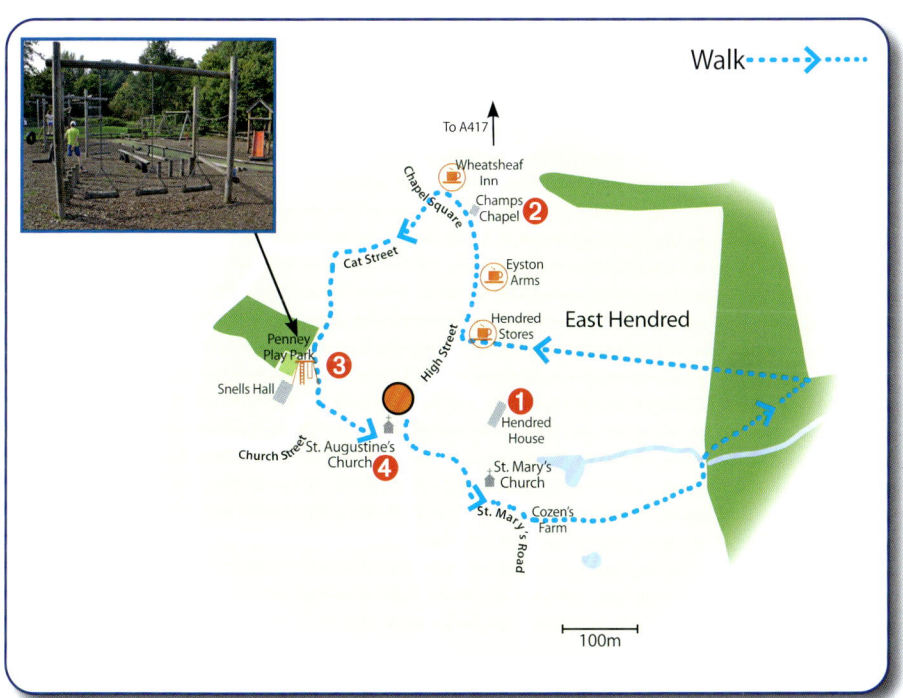

East Hendred

Facts and Figures

1. Hendred House has been owned by the same family, the Eystons, since the mid-1400s. That part of East Hendred to the east of High Street was associated with Catholicism, including this manor house and estate, St Mary's church and St Amand's school. There is a centuries-old custom of village children converging on Hendred House on Shrove Tuesday to receive a currant bun and a halfpenny (now one new penny).

2. Champs Chapel Museum is a small village museum housed in the former Chapel of Jesus of Bethlehem, built in 1453 by Carthusian monks. It opens on Sunday afternoons from April to October (www.hendredmuseum.org.uk).

3. The Penney Playpark was opened in 2000 by Lady Penney in memory of her husband William, Baron Penney of East Hendred, a physicist who played a leading role in Britain's nuclear programme.

4. The church of St Augustine of Canterbury was built in the late 12th century, with the tower dating from 1450. The clock (thought to be from 1525) is faceless, instead using the six church bells to call out the quarters and hours and playing the 'Angel's Song' (by Orlando Gibbons) at midday and every third hour. Among the church's treasures is a fine 13th century lectern.

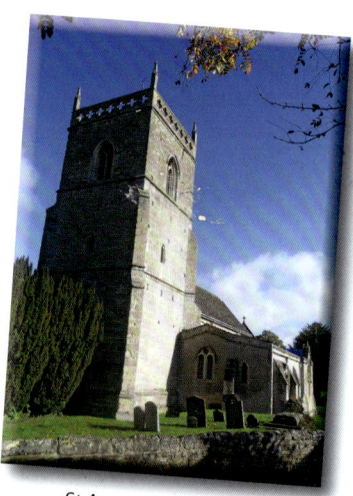

St Augustine's Church

Can you find the face in the wall?

Wooden Owl Sculpture

WALK FIVE : EWELME

Explore this historic village, set beside a clear stream on the edge of the Chilterns (*Midsomer Murders* location).

START/PARKING: Recreation Ground car park (free), Cow Common at the eastern end of Ewelme, about 3 miles NE of Wallingford between the A4130 and B4009 (Nat Grid Ref 41/648912, Postcode OX10 6PG)
PUBLIC TRANSPORT: Thames Travel bus route 136 from Cholsey and Wallingford, Mon-Sat, stops near the Shepherd's Hut at the western end of Ewelme
DISTANCE: ¾ mile (1¼ km) or 2 miles (3¼ km)
REFRESHMENTS: Village Store (www.ewelmevillagestore.co.uk) and the Shepherd's Hut pub, with a garden (www.shepherdshutewelme.co.uk)
PUBLIC TOILETS: None, but toilets at the Shepherd's Hut and Village Store for customers
PATHS: Mainly village roads, but the longer route involves footpaths that are unsuitable for pushchairs and liable to be muddy after wet weather.

THE ROUTES: The walks start at the Recreation Ground, which has wooden play equipment suitable for primary and pre-school children. From the car park, cross the road by the grass triangle with a signpost and take the higher road on your left (Parson's Lane). Follow this road to reach Ewelme parish church ❶ on the left. It is well worth visiting this beautiful building and the courtyard of the neighbouring almshouses ❷, reached through a wooden door and down steps in a covered passageway opposite the west door of the church.

From the church, follow the road gently downhill, turning left at the T-junction (care needed as there is no pavement). Continuing downhill, the King's Pool ❸ is on your left and the Village Store ❹ on the right, with a village map on the wall nearby. For the shorter route, turn left here into The Street – note the old sign about the Ewelme Brook on the wall of Day's Cottage shortly on the right. Follow the road ahead to pass Ewelme primary school, considered to be the oldest in England, and the Recreation Ground and car park are reached on the right.

For the longer route, turn right at the King's Pool and follow The Street. Running parallel to the road is the Ewelme Brook, a clear chalk stream that once fed extensive watercress beds. The Watercress Beds Visitor Centre ❺ is reached on the left, from where a grassy path runs beside the water. Follow this, then rejoin The Street to reach the Shepherd's Hut pub and turn left here (care needed as

Ewelme

there is no pavement). On the right just before a bridge is the entrance to a nature reserve and the site of an old mill, with an information panel. Carefully cross the bridge and turn left into Green Lane. Just past a bus stop, take the permissive footpath on the left and follow this along a field edge for about 800m. At the far side of the field, where the path bears right, turn left on to a narrow path that runs downhill between trees then gardens. On reaching The Street, turn right and then follow the shorter route (page 17).

No spoiling the brook sign!

Ewelme Primary School

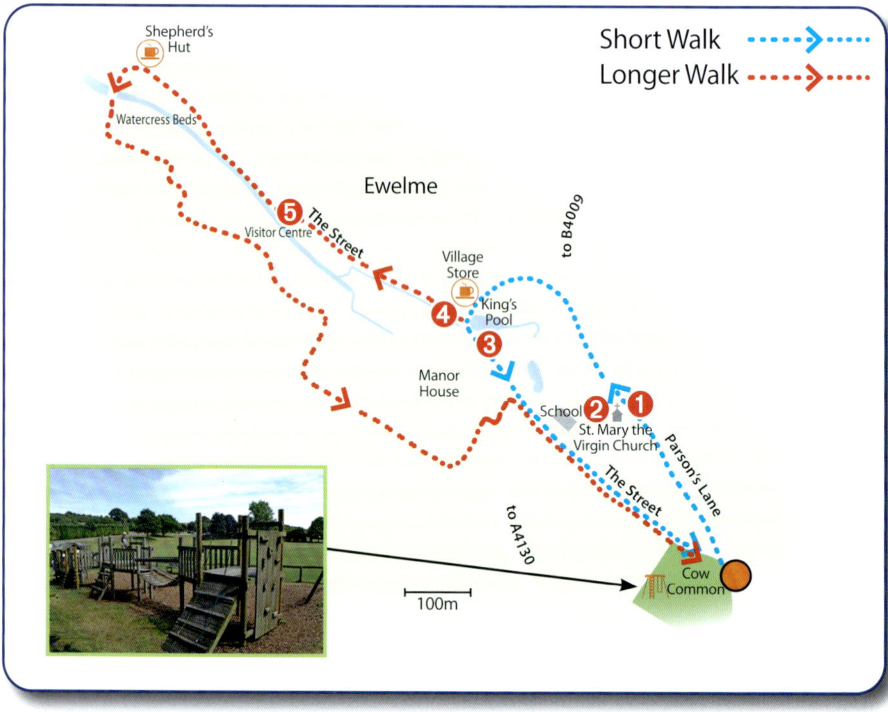

Facts and Figures

❶ The tower of the large and attractive church of St Mary the Virgin is 14th century and the remainder dates from the 15th. Among the many interesting features are the large carved wooden cover for the font and the magnificent 15th century alabaster tomb of Alice, Duchess of Suffolk. The grave of Jerome K Jerome, author of the Thames adventure *Three Men in a Boat*, is south-east of the church (near the path to the Old Rectory).

❷ The cloistered almshouses were established in 1437 by the Duke and Duchess of Suffolk using profits from the East Anglian wool trade. The original thirteen almshouses have been reduced to eight, but are still run as a charity by the Ewelme Trust.

❸ The attractive King's Pool is fed by a spring just north of the village – tradition has it that Henry VIII bathed here when staying at nearby Ewelme Manor. The Ewelme Brook flows out of the pool down through the village.

❹ Ewelme Village Store, housed in the former Wesleyan chapel of 1826, is run by volunteers and includes a Tea Room (www.ewelmevillagestore.co.uk).

❺ The Watercress Beds Visitor Centre opens on the first Sunday each month. From the late 1800s, the clear, fast running Ewelme Brook was used extensively for the cultivation of watercress. However, greater competition and regulation led to production ceasing in 1988. The Chiltern Society purchased the beds and established a conservation programme and local nature reserve (www.ewelmewatercressbeds.org).

St Mary the Virgin Church   *King's Pool*

WALK SIX : HENLEY-ON-THAMES

Follow the towpath through this beautiful Thames-side resort to a lock busy with boats (*Midsomer Murders* location).

START/PARKING: Car park at Henley-on-Thames rail station (pay and display), off Station Road (Nat Grid Ref 41/763823, Postcode RG9 1AY). Alternative (more expensive) pay and display parking at Mill Meadows, Meadow Road off Station Road (Postcode RG9 1BF)
PUBLIC TRANSPORT: Henley-on-Thames rail station; buses to town centre from Reading, Wallingford, Oxford and High Wycombe
DISTANCE: 2 miles (3¼ km), but the walk is 'there and back' so may be shortened
REFRESHMENTS: Henley Piazza café, Mill Meadows; Chocolate Café, Thames Side; Café at River and Rowing Museum; several coffee shops and pubs in town centre
PUBLIC TOILETS: Station car park and Mill Meadows (octagonal pavilion)
PATHS: Pavements and riverside footpath, level and suitable for pushchairs (but may be flooded when the Thames is high)

THE ROUTE: From the Station car park, turn right into Station Road and follow this down to the river. There is a fine view of Henley Bridge ❶, with the regatta course beyond. Turn right along the riverside path, to pass Hobbs of Henley who provide boat trips and boat hire, and enter Mill Meadows. There are information panels on the right about the riverside and the stone Henley Obelisk, now here but originally erected in the Market Place in the late 1700s. Facilities at Mill Meadows include a café, plenty of benches and space for picnics and two children's playgrounds – one for pre-school and younger primary ages and another with wooden equipment suitable for older children. The attractive river scene is usually busy with boats and water birds, against a backdrop of islands and wooded hills on the Berkshire side.

Follow the riverside path, passing the River and Rowing Museum ❷, to reach the broad grassy expanse of Marsh Meadows. These have small ponds and reed beds, with a wildlife trail that leaves the riverside path just beyond the museum. Continue along the path for about another

Henley-on-Thames

600m to Mill Lane. Bear left here on to a wooden footbridge, towards the foaming water of Marsh Weir, to reach Marsh Lock ❸. There are several benches here to sit and watch people 'messing about in boats' and an information board about the fish ladders at the side of the weir. The wooden bridge beyond the lock leads back to the Oxfordshire bank.

To complete the walk, return along the footbridge and the riverside path, passing Marsh Meadows and Mill Meadows again, as far as the 'Angel on the Bridge' pub by Henley Bridge. Nearby Hart Street leads to the parish church of St Mary the Virgin ❹ and the town centre, which are both well worth exploring. Otherwise, return to Station Road and the start of the walk.

"Believe me, my young friend, there is nothing – absolutely nothing – half so much worth doing as simply messing about in boats" - Ratty to Mole in "The Wind in the Willows" by Kenneth Grahame

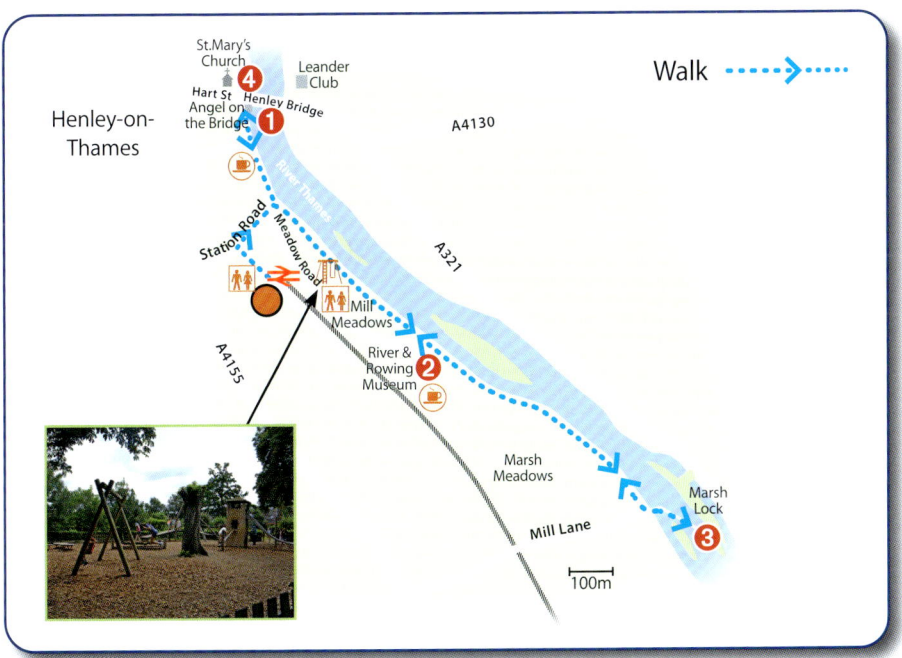

Henley-on-Thames

Facts and Figures

❶ The attractive Henley Bridge, with its five arches, was completed in 1786. The original bridge was built slightly upstream around 1170 and its two stone abutments are still standing, one underpinning the front of the 'Angel on the Bridge' pub. The central arch has two carvings of mythical river figures – Isis looking upstream and Tamesis downstream. Just downstream on the Berkshire bank is the prestigious Leander Club, the home of British rowing. Beyond this is the straight 2km course of the Royal Regatta, held each summer.

❷ The museum has galleries dedicated to rowing, the non-tidal Thames, Henley and *The Wind in the Willows* (www.rrm.co.uk). In the car park is an impressive bronze sculpture of Olympic gold medallist rowers Steve Redgrave and Matthew Pinsent, both Leander Club members.

❸ A pound lock was first built here in 1773 and has been re-built several times, the latest being in 2004. Because it is on the opposite side of the river from the towpath, it was considered 'inconvenient and dangerous for barges' and long bridges were built to carry the path to the lock and back – a unique feature on the Thames.

❹ St Mary's church is basically a 13th century building that was enlarged in the 15th and 19th centuries; its fine tower dates from the mid-1500s. Next door is the Chantry House, thought to have been built around 1450 by a wealthy merchant, later to become a school. In the churchyard is a memorial stone to the 1960s singer Dusty Springfield, a Henley resident.

Sculpture of Redgrave and Pinsent

St Mary's Church and River

WALK SEVEN : SOUTH STOKE

A Thames-side walk from this picturesque village to a marvel of Victorian engineering.

START/PARKING: At the Recreation Ground off Cross Keys Road, South Stoke. There is a small, free car park here and ample roadside parking nearby in The Street. South Stoke lies close to the B4009 about 2 miles north of Goring-on-Thames (Nat Grid Ref 41/602836, Postcode RG8 0JT)
PUBLIC TRANSPORT: Going Forward bus route 134 Wallingford to Goring-on-Thames, Mon-Fri
DISTANCE: 2 miles (3¼ km)
REFRESHMENTS: Community Shop by the Recreation Ground (open Mon-Sat and Sun morning); Perch and Pike Inn, with a garden (www.perchandpike.co.uk)
PUBLIC TOILETS: None, but toilets at the Perch and Pike for customers
PATHS: Village roads and level footpaths; the paths are unsuitable for pushchairs and liable to be muddy after wet weather. The riverside path may be flooded when the Thames is high.

THE ROUTE: The Recreation Ground has a spacious, well-equipped children's playground with seats and picnic tables. To begin the walk, turn right into Cross Keys Road and pass under the railway bridge to reach The Street. There are village information boards by the junction. Turn right, passing the attractive 17th century Perch and Pike Inn, the village school and St Andrew's church ❶ on the right. At the end of The Street turn left into Ferry Lane, signposted 'Ridgeway'. Bearing left, following a sign 'To the river', join a track bordered by trees that leads to the Thames. There is a seat here, by the site of the former ferry to Moulsford on the opposite bank, and an information panel about the Ridgeway National Trail ❷.

To continue the walk, turn right through a metal gate to join the riverside path. The river is usually busy with rowers training and with pleasure craft in summer. Shortly, there are views of a church and then a marina on the Moulsford side and of a railway embankment ahead. The path leads to an impressive brick railway bridge ❸ spanning the river. After admiring this fine example of Victorian engineering, re-trace your steps back to South Stoke*. Turn right into The Street and at St Andrew's pass through the lych

23

South Stoke

gate and take the path towards the church. By the entrance, bear right and follow the path ahead by walls to reach Cross Keys Road. Turn left here and, immediately after the bridge, steps on the left lead to a path into the Recreation Ground.

Alternatively, for a circular walk of about 2¾ miles in total, pass under the railway bridge and continue along the riverside path. This eventually leads to another former ferry, at Little Stoke. Turn right here at a 'Ridgeway' sign then go straight on following a footpath sign to join a gravel drive that leads past Little Stoke House. Passing the thatched School House on the left, continue along a track to reach a narrow lane and turn right here. This leads past Little Stoke Manor Farm and at the far end of a flint wall, where the lane turns to the left, go ahead over a stone stile to join a footpath. This crosses a field, with stiles at each end, to a small wooden bridge. The path then veers slightly left to reach a tunnel, the 'Bogey Hole', under the railway. On the far side, the path continues left across a field to reach cottages on the edge of South Stoke. Turn right at Ferry Road, then left into The Street. At St Andrew's, pass through the lych gate and take the path towards the church. By the entrance, bear right and follow the path ahead by walls to reach Cross Keys Road. Turn left here and, immediately after the bridge, steps on the left lead to a path into the Recreation Ground.

Facts and Figures

❶ Flint-faced St Andrew's parish church dates from the early 13th century, although the tower is probably 15th century, and is especially interesting for it's decorated memorials. Oliver Cromwell stabled his horses here during the siege of Wallingford in the English Civil War, mid-1600s.

❷ The 87 mile Ridgeway Trail runs from near Avebury in Wiltshire to the Thames at the Goring Gap. It then follows the river northwards through South Stoke before swinging east then north-east through the Chilterns to Ivinghoe Beacon in Buckinghamshire.

❸ Moulsford railway bridge is a pair of parallel bridges designed by Isambard Kingdom Brunel for the Great Western Railway from London to Bristol. The original (downstream) one was built in 1838-39 and the first passenger train crossed it on 1 June 1840, when the section from Reading to Steventon opened. The second bridge was added in 1892 when the line was doubled. The brickwork was 'fanned' to suit the skewed arches.

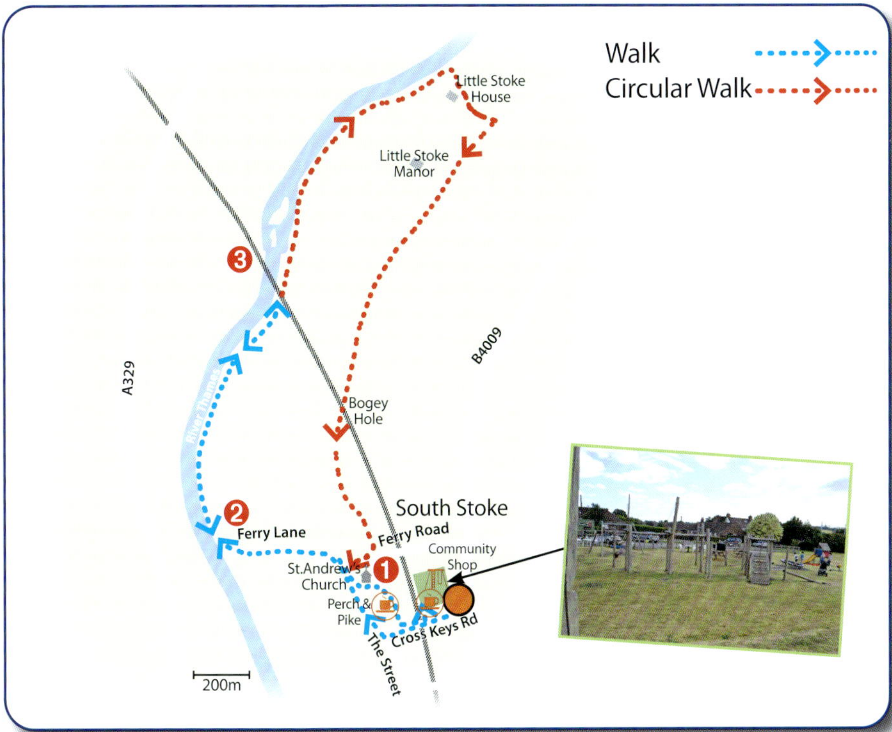

South Stoke

Moulsford Railway Bridge

St Andrew's Church

Pub Sign

25

WALK EIGHT : STADHAMPTON

Circular walks from an animal farm to explore an historic country estate.

START/PARKING: Car park at the Crazy Bear Farm Shop, Newells Lane off the A329 on the southern edge of Stadhampton, about 7 miles SE of Oxford (Nat Grid Ref 41/605981, Postcode OX44 7XJ). This is open daily until 6pm
PUBLIC TRANSPORT: Thames Travel bus route 11 from Oxford to Watlington
DISTANCE: 1¼ miles (2 km) or 1¾ miles (2¾ km)
REFRESHMENTS: Crazy Bear Farm Shop (www.crazybeargroup.co.uk); The Crown pub (www.the-crown.pub); M&S food store at BP petrol station
PUBLIC TOILETS: None, but toilets at the Farm Shop and The Crown for customers
PATHS: Level tracks and footpaths but with several stiles and liable to be muddy after wet weather, so mostly unsuitable for pushchairs

THE ROUTES: Near the Crazy Bear Farm Shop are paddocks with various animals, including llamas, chickens, goats and pigs, and children's play equipment. To begin the walk, go along the stony track running past the Farm Shop and at the far end turn left near a small lake. Follow a path, with the lake on your right and a stream to the left, then over a small bridge so that the stream is on the right. This leads to a stile at the edge of Ascott Park ❶. An information panel introduces the Ascott Park Historical Trail, which the route now follows.

Follow the broad grassy path ahead to another stile and a panel (no. 3) describing features of the park here, such as fishponds. Continue across the grass towards the octagonal, red brick dovecot, just beyond and to the left of which is information panel no. 4. Inside the walls are the nesting holes the doves used. From here, turn right across the grass to another panel (no. 5) at what may have been the intended site of the house. Then continue ahead to panel 6, describing the thatched building to your right. From here, turn left across the grass to reach a stile and just beyond is panel 7, giving information about the stone gate piers ahead. There is a further panel (no. 8) close to these piers. Returning to panel 7 and the stile, bear right towards panel 5 and the dovecot. Passing this on your left, continue ahead along the grassy path then bear right towards a stile at the field corner.

After the stile, there is a choice of routes. For a shorter walk, turn left along a path that leads back to the end of the track from the Farm Shop. To continue to Stadhampton village green with its children's playground, take the footpath ahead across a field. At the far side, go ahead along a path bordered by garden fences, at the end of which bear right on to a lane to the nearby village green ❷. Here there are benches and wooden play equipment for primary and pre-school children.

Continue along the edge of the green past cottages then, just past Long Barn and The Stables, turn left down a lane. Follow this to the gates of The Mill House, then turn right along a narrow footpath leading to the main road. Turn left here to pass a (colourfully decorated) bus shelter, the shop and petrol station. Just beyond, by a post box, turn left between cottages. A left turn into Bear Lane and a right turn at the Crazy Bear Hotel leads to Newells Lane and the start of the walk.

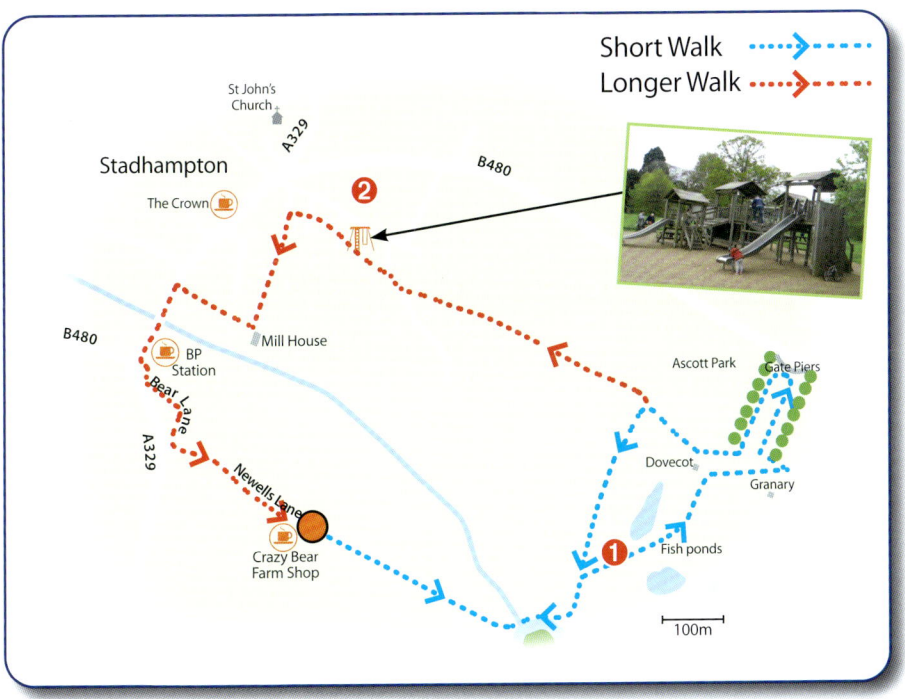

Stadhampton

Facts and Figures

❶ Ascott Park was the estate of the Dormer family who built a manor house here in the early 1500s. After this was damaged in the English Civil War, a new house was built but shortly after completion in 1662 this burned down. Although gardens and avenues of trees were laid out in the early 1700s, the Dormers fell into debt and the house was never re-built. Oxfordshire County Council (OCC) acquired Ascott shortly after WW1 to provide agricultural holdings for returning soldiers. After WW2, much of the estate was sold to tenants but the land surrounding the former house was retained by OCC.

❷ The large village green, bisected by the Oxford to Henley road, is bordered by cottages and the attractive parish church of St John the Baptist. There has been a church here since at least the 12th century, restored and enlarged several times, the last time being 1875.

St John's Church

Ascott Park Dovecote

Llamas at Crazy Bear

WALK NINE : STOKE ROW

Discover a taste of India in this small village high in the Chilterns (*Midsomer Murders* location).

START/PARKING: Car park (free) behind Stoke Row Village Hall on the corner of Main Street and Benares Grove, or roadside nearby. Stoke Row lies midway between Wallingford and Henley about 2 miles south of the A4130 (Nat Grid Ref 41/679840, Postcode RG9 5QH)
PUBLIC TRANSPORT: Going Forward buses from Goring to Henley (only limited journeys on Thursdays at time of publication)
DISTANCE: 1½ miles (2½ km) or 1¾ miles (2¾ km)
REFRESHMENTS: Stoke Row Store with coffee shop and takeaway (www.stokerowstore.co.uk); Cherry Tree Inn (www.thecherrytreeinn.co.uk) and Crooked Billet Inn (www.thecrookedbillet.co.uk)
PUBLIC TOILETS: None, but toilets at the pubs for customers
PATHS: Village roads and footpaths. The paths are liable to be muddy after wet weather and are unsuitable for pushchairs.

THE ROUTE: From the Village Hall, cross the road and a few metres along to the left is the ornate Maharajah's Well ❶, set in a small garden with benches and information panels. Next to this is the octagonal Well Cottage, previously used by the Well Warden. To start the walk, return to Main Street and turn left past Well Cottage Garden. Ignoring the signed footpath, turn left through a gate into the Cherry Orchard ❷. From the information panel walk across the grass, with the road to your right, then bear left towards a well-equipped children's playground. Then bear slightly left along a grassy path between an elephant statue on the bandstand mound and a pond, to reach a gate in the far corner. Turn right here then right into Cox's Lane and follow this back to Main Street.

Turn left and follow Main Street before turning left into Nottwood Lane at a crossroads. Follow this lane to a corner with a metal gate to a footpath on the left. This path borders the gardens of Rose Cottage and leads through another metal gate to a paddock (note the plaques by the gate dedicated to *'a gentle Guernsey house cow'* and *'a placid Gloucester Old Spot sow who reared 71 lovely porkers'*). At the far corner of the paddock is a covered brick gateway with seats. After pausing here to admire the lovely view of rolling fields and woods, retrace your steps to Nottwood Lane and then turn left.

The lane leads to the attractive Crooked Billet Inn ❸. Just beyond here, there is the option of a woodland detour (involving an uphill climb). Turn left down the drive to Bushwood House then, by gates, take the footpath to the right into Bush Wood. Where paths cross, continue ahead downhill then, a few metres before reaching a small road, take the path to the right uphill. Where this reaches Newlands Lane, turn left and follow the lane to reach the village green. Turn right here along the road, passing Stoke Row chapel then the Cherry Tree Inn. The road then leads past the Stoke Row Store on the left to arrive back at the start.

Stoke Row

Facts and Figures

❶ As the inscription on the well's gilded dome states, it was a gift from the Maharajah of Benares in 1864. Construction was organised by Mr Edward Reade of nearby Ipsden, who had told the Maharajah of the plight of the villagers when their water sources dried up in summer. Stoke Row is one of the highest villages in the Chilterns - about 550 ft above sea level - and the well had to be 368 ft deep (about twice the height of Nelson's Column!). It was dug by hand and lined with bricks – a remarkable feat that took about a year to complete. The well was used until the 1930s, by when pipelines had arrived to provide a public water supply.

❷ The Maharajah also paid for a cottage for the well warden and a four acre cherry orchard to provide a source of income, following the Indian tradition of a free well being financed by a fruit harvest. As well as cherry trees, this orchard ('Ishree Bagh') has a pond, a shady ravine and a bandstand mound. It is now used for village events.

❸ The Crooked Billet, built in 1642, was once the hideout of highwayman Dick Turpin who was romantically attached to the landlord's daughter. Chef Paul Clerehugh took over as landlord in 1989 and has won numerous food awards; actress Kate Winslet chose the pub for her wedding reception in 1997.

The Crooked Billet Inn

Sign at The Crooked Billet

Maharajah's Well and Well Cottage

WALK TEN: THE HANNEYS

Explore this pair of Vale villages, divided by a pretty chalk stream with an industrial past.

START/PARKING: Car park (free) at the Hanney War Memorial Hall, Brookside, East Hanney off the A338 about 3 miles north of Wantage (Nat Grid Ref 41/414929, Postcode OX12 0JL)
PUBLIC TRANSPORT: Stagecoach buses from Wantage, Abingdon and Oxford; Thames Travel buses from Wantage and Didcot to East Hanney
DISTANCE: 1¾ miles (2¾ km)
REFRESHMENTS: Hanney Community Shop (Mon-Sat to 5pm); The Plough, West Hanney (closed Mon, www.theploughatwesthanney.co.uk) and The Black Horse, East Hanney (www.blackhorseeasthanney.co.uk)
PUBLIC TOILETS: None, but toilets at the pubs for customers
PATHS: Village roads and footpaths. The paths are liable to be muddy after wet weather and are unsuitable for pushchairs.

THE ROUTE: Next to the car park off Brookside is a children's playground suitable for pre-school and primary ages and the Hanney Community Shop selling drinks and ice creams.

To begin the walk, turn left at the corner into Brookside - it's namesake, Letcombe Brook, is seen shortly on the left. Go over the bridge (care needed, as the pavement and bridge are narrow) to the former Dandridge's Mill ❶. This building has been converted into apartments, for which power is generated by an Archimedean Hydro Screw using the mill race. Cross back over the bridge and take the public footpath to the left by the Old Mill House. Go through a farmyard and a kissing gate then follow the grassy path ahead along the field edge (electrified fencing is sometimes used here). After another gate, cross over a track then through a gate and ahead along another field edge to a pair of gates. That on the left leads to Community Woodland but go through the one on the right, leading into the churchyard of St James the Great, the ancient parish church of West Hanney ❷.

In front of the church is an attractive group of buildings, including imposing West Hanney House ahead. Close by to the left is The Plough, a 17th century

The Hanneys

thatched pub with a beer garden. To continue the walk, from the church go ahead along the raised (uneven) stone pavement of Church Street to the village green, with the stone Butter Cross. From here, cross the road into Winter Lane opposite (care needed after the pavement finishes). Follow this to where it curves to the right then join a footpath on the right that runs across the middle of a large field. There are open views to the distant Berkshire Downs to the south and hills near Oxford to the north. At the far side of the field, go through a gate and turn left on to a track. Shortly, by a metal gate, take a footpath to the right. Towards the end of this, another former grain mill comes into view – Lower Mill. Cross the bridge over Letcombe Brook and take the footpath to the left of the Mill, going through a metal gate.

This path follows the winding brook, passing a wooden bench with an intriguing inscription ❸; an information panel is nearby. Where the path forks, near a cottage, take the path to the right to stay near the brook. This leads to a picnic table and bench by an iron bridge. Go over this bridge and the path then leads past allotments back to the start.

The Hanneys

Facts and Figures

❶ Dandridge's Mill was built about 1820 as a silk mill. It became a grain mill in 1839 and milling continued until the 1930s. During WW2, it was a small engineering works producing aircraft parts. Conversion to apartments took place in 2008.

❷ The first church here was Saxon, but little remains of this apart from two Saxon stone coffins in the North Porch. Much of the present building dates from 1160 and is a fine example of a Norman church. The original central tower was replaced by one on the north side in the late 12th century, but this was found to be unsafe in the early 1900s when it was replaced by the present shorter bell tower. On the north wall is a memorial to Elizabeth Bowles, considered the oldest person to have lived in England; she died in 1718 at the alleged age of 124.

❸ The inscription on this bench, "Ore stabit fortis arare placet ore stat", appears to be Latin but is actually 'pseudo Latin' - it should be read as "O rest a bit for tis a rare place to rest at"! The Letcombe Brook that the bench overlooks is a chalk stream flowing from the Berkshire Downs south-west of Wantage.

The Plough

St. James the Great Church

West Hanney sign post

WALK ELEVEN: WALLINGFORD

Discover over 1000 years of history on the banks of the Thames (*Midsomer Murders* location).

START/PARKING: Riverside Park, reached via Stephen's Field near the eastern end of Wallingford Bridge (Nat Grid Ref 41/611895, Postcode OX10 8EB). The pay and display car park here is free after 3pm on Saturday and all day Sunday
PUBLIC TRANSPORT: Thames Travel buses from Oxford, Didcot, Henley and Reading
DISTANCE: Castle route 1¼ miles (2 km); Bull Croft route 1½ miles (2½ km)
REFRESHMENTS: Various cafes, shops and pubs, including the Boat House by the bridge and the Coach and Horses, Kine Croft. Café at Riverside Park when pool open (summer)
PUBLIC TOILETS: Riverside Park (April-Sept) and Waitrose car park, High Street
PATHS: Pavements and footpaths; the riverside and meadow paths are liable to be muddy after wet weather (and flooded when the Thames is high)

THE ROUTES: The Riverside Park has plenty of space for picnics, a children's water play area and an open air swimming pool (summer). There are good views of the river and the town opposite. Nearby is a well-equipped children's playground, at Crowmarsh Gifford Recreation Ground.

To start the walk, go up on to Wallingford Bridge ❶ via either the (steep!) steps near the river or the car park entrance. After crossing the bridge, turn right just past the Boat House pub into Castle Lane then immediately right behind the pub along a gravel path to the Thames. There is an information panel here and several seats to pause and watch any passing boats. The path soon borders grassy meadows to the left – the site of Wallingford Castle ❷, of which only earthworks and a few walls remain. Shortly after going over a wooden footbridge, turn left through a metal gate into the meadows. There is information here about the Castle Meadows and the Castle Gardens. Take the path ahead across the meadow to reach a wooden gate. Just beyond, there are two walk options – either a route through the Castle Gardens (when open, see ❷) that allows a closer look at the castle remains or one to the Bull Croft via a section of Saxon earthworks – see page 37.

CASTLE ROUTE: Bear left across the grass to join a stony path that soon reaches a gate on the left leading to a pond with an information panel about this wildlife haven. A few steps lead to another gate, turning right to rejoin the path. Near the remains of the Queen's Tower is a panel to help visualise the layout of this enormous castle. Continue along a grassy path (at the edge of the Inner Bailey) to pass a bench where the tree-covered mound of the castle motte is to your left. The grassy path leads round to a wooden kissing gate, where there is another information panel, and the entrance to the gardens. These have plenty of seats, grassy slopes, views and fine trees! To climb the motte and take in the views over the town and river, turn left over the grass to a wooden bridge that leads to a zig-zag path up the mound.

To continue the walk, from the gardens entrance go ahead down a slope then bear left across the grass past a small ornamental pond to reach a gate in the wall. Turn right here into Bear Lane, where there is an interesting panel about All Hallows churchyard and the George Hotel. Turn left into Castle Street and carefully cross this before turning right at the cross-roads. After about 100m, the entrance to the Bull Croft is on the right. There are two children's playgrounds here, one for pre-school and younger primary ages and another for older children a little further on the left. The remains of Saxon ramparts ❸ may be found at the far side of the park. The route is then the same as that after the Bull Croft (see below).

BULL CROFT ROUTE: Just beyond the gate at Castle Meadows, bear right across the grass towards a brick wall to reach a wooden kissing gate and then turn left into Cemetery Lane. At the end of the lane, carefully cross the road and turn left along the pavement. After passing the entrance to Park Farm House and just before The Old School House, turn right down a few steps on to a narrow, shady footpath. This leads to the ditch and bank that are the remains of part of Saxon ramparts ❸; there is an information panel by the path. At the end of the path turn left into St Georges Road then after about 100m, turn left into a park - the Bull Croft. An optional alternative is to turn left just before the road, down into the ditch and over the bank (a very steep slope!) to enter the Bull Croft. Head diagonally across the grass to reach two children's playgrounds, one suited to pre-school and younger primary ages and one for older children.

Leave the Bull Croft through the gateway beyond the playgrounds and turn right into High Street to reach the 15th century Flint House, now Wallingford Museum ❹. Carefully cross the road here to enter another, smaller park – the Kine Croft – which is also bounded on two sides by the remains of Saxon ramparts. Bear left across the grass towards the Coach and Horses pub, passing an information panel, and then turn left into Kine Croft. Carefully cross Goldsmith's Lane to enter Church Lane which soon leads to the parish church of St Mary-le-More and the attractive Market Place ❺.

To return to the start, leave the Market Place via narrow St Mary's Street then turn right into High Street, carefully crossing the road to reach the Bridge.

Wallingford

Facts and Figures

❶ When William the Conqueror and his army crossed the Thames here in 1066, before marching on London, they used a ford and, presumably, boats. A bridge was first recorded in 1141. The present one dates from the early 1800s and is about 300m long with 19 arches.

❷ The Normans began to build the castle in 1067 and it was later expanded to become one of the most powerful and impressive in England. During the English Civil War it was a royalist stronghold but in 1646 the castle fell to the Parliamentarians, who ordered its demolition in 1652. The gardens are open daily, to 6pm Apr-May, 7pm Jun-Sept and 3pm Oct-Mar (see www.wallingford.co.uk).

❸ The Saxon earthworks date from the 9th century, when King Alfred built a fortified town to help defend Wessex from the Vikings. These fortifications enclosed the town on three sides, the Thames providing defence to the east. They had a water-filled outer ditch and were probably capped by a wooden palisade. Over time, the banks have been eroded to about two-thirds of their original height.

❹ The museum tells the story of Wallingford and is open from March to November (see www.wallingfordmuseum.org.uk)

❺ The Market Place has been the heart of the town since Saxon times and the Charter Market is held here every Friday, as it has been for over 850 years. The handsome Town Hall dates from 1670 and behind this is the church of St Mary-le-More, largely Victorian but with a tower built in 1653 partly using stone from Wallingford Castle. On the east side is the Corn Exchange, dating from 1856, now a theatre and cinema.

View from Riverside Park

Town Hall

WALK TWELVE : WATLINGTON

Two walks – one to discover this attractive market town, another climbing into the Chilterns to see panoramic views (*Midsomer Murders* location).

START/PARKING: For the Town route, the (free) car park at the Recreation Ground, off the B4009 close to the northern edge of Watlington (Nat Grid Ref 41/691948, Postcode OX49 5BZ). For the Hill route, the (free) Town car park in Hill Road (Nat Grid Ref 41/691945, Postcode OX49 5AD)
PUBLIC TRANSPORT: Thames Travel bus route 11 from Oxford
DISTANCE: Town route ¾ mile (1¼ km); Hill route 2 miles (3¼ km)
REFRESHMENTS: Granary Delicatessen in High Street (open Mon – Sat); the Fat Fox Inn, The Chequers and Spire and Spoke pubs; Co-op store (open daily)
PUBLIC TOILETS: Church Street
PATHS: The Town route is along level paths and pavements, suitable for pushchairs. The Hill route involves footpaths that may be muddy after wet weather and a steep climb and descent

TOWN ROUTE: Watlington Recreation Ground has a well-equipped children's playground, suitable for ages up to about 12 years, a skate park and an adult 'outdoor gym'. To begin the walk, go past the outdoor gym equipment and leave the Recreation Ground by a path that leads to Love Lane. Turn left here then right into Shirburn Street (B4009). After passing the Fat Fox Inn, the town centre is soon reached.

At the brick-built Town Hall ❶, turn right into High Street. This has a wealth of interesting 15th, 16th and 17th century buildings including several former pubs (e.g. numbers 12, 15 and 17) and the timber Granary on staddle stones for grain storage. At the far end on the right is the War Memorial, winner of prizes for being the best kept in Oxfordshire. Just beyond, turn right into Chapel Street, to pass the thatched Black Horse Cottage. At the next thatched cottage, turn left into New Road (the 16th century Chequers pub lies a little further along Chapel Street). At the end of New Road is Church Street; the ancient parish church of St Leonards is about 200m to the right from here. To continue the walk, turn left into Church Street then left into High Street. At the War Memorial, cross the road and take the access road by the Library. This leads to The Paddock, an attractive small park with seats and play equipment for pre-school children. On returning to the High Street,

Watlington

turn right towards the Town Hall. To complete the walk, re-trace your steps along Shirburn Street and Love Lane to the Recreation Ground.

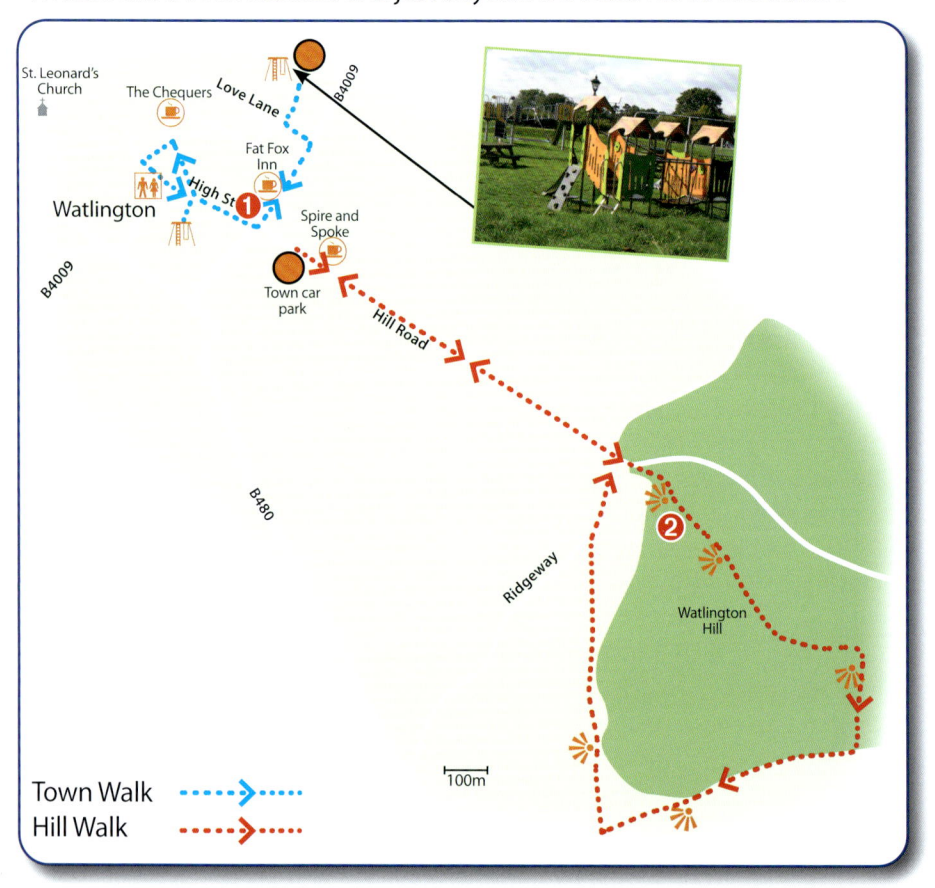

HILL ROUTE: For a walk up Watlington Hill, from the Town car park turn right into Hill Road; the Spire and Spoke pub will be found shortly on the left. Follow Hill Road as it gently rises towards the Chiltern escarpment – there are fine views of this across fields to the left and Red Kites are often calling overhead! Just beyond the Watlington sign, the White Mark ❷ comes into view on the hillside ahead. About 10m beyond where the Ridgeway trail crosses the road, take the footpath to the right. This path climbs steeply and may be slippery after wet weather, but the effort is well worth it! The White Mark is soon reached and just beyond is a bench to sit and admire the panoramic view across the Vale and along the escarpment. The chalky grassland of 738 ft (225m) high Watlington Hill is a Site of Special Scientific Interest, home to large numbers of wild flowers, butterflies and birds.

Continue uphill to a level area and, on reaching a wooden post by the path, turn right across the grass. There are further great views as this grassy path goes steeply downhill. At the bottom of the slope, turn right on to a footpath. This meanders gently down by yew woodland (with more fine views!) to reach a kissing gate then two wooden gates with a narrow track between. Turn right here through a metal field gate to join a permissive path over a grassy field. Go straight ahead, with woods to the right and wide views to the left. At the far field edge, go through a wooden gate and turn right to join a track (the Ridgeway). Shortly this leads to Hill Road - turn left here to return to Watlington.

Facts and Figures

❶ The attractive gabled Town Hall was built in 1664-65 as a market hall with a boy's school above and is now used for meetings and social events.

❷ The White Mark is a large obelisk shape, 82m long, cut into the chalk. It is believed to have been carved in 1764 so that, seen from west of Watlington, it creates the illusion of a spire on top of the tower of St Leonard's parish church.

The White Mark

Town Hall

Further Information

Some useful websites to help you plan and enjoy the walks.

MET OFFICE
www.metoffice.gov.uk
Local weather forecasts for up to 7 days ahead.

ORDNANCE SURVEY
www.ordnancesurvey.co.uk
Mapping services, including online access to Landranger and Pathfinder maps.

THAMES TRAVEL BUSES
www.thames-travel.co.uk
Maps and timetables for buses in South Oxfordshire.

GOING FORWARD BUSES
www.goingforwardbuses.com
Bus timetables for South Oxfordshire.

GREAT WESTERN RAILWAY TRAINS
www.gwr.com
Timetables, tickets and train running information.

SOUTHERN OXFORDSHIRE TOURISM
www.southernoxfordshire.com
Things to see and do in South Oxfordshire and Vale of White Horse.

THE CHILTERNS AREA OF OUTSTANDING NATURAL BEAUTY (AONB)
www.chilternsaonb.org
Visitor guide, maps, news and events across the AONB.

MIDSOMER MURDERS
www.midsomermurders.org
The real-life locations used for TV's *Midsomer Murders*.

GEOCACHING
www.geocaching.com
Treasure hunting using a GPS receiver to seek hidden small containers with logbooks and items such as toys and trinkets. There are 'geocaches' on or close to all the walks.